I0414237

BY THE PEOPLE, FOR THE PEOPLE

American Politics. A Lost Cause? Or A Time For Change?

"DO NOT FIX WHAT IS

NOT BROKEN!

BUT WHEN IT IS BROKEN, GET OFF
YOUR REAR AND FIX IT!"

~ Francis Elder II

BY THE PEOPLE, FOR THE PEOPLE

American Politics. A Lost
Cause Or A Time For Change?

© Francis Elder II
PO Box 782   Kansas, OK 74347
frank@booksbyelder.com

2nd Edition November 2016

This work may not be reproduced, copied or re-distributed in
any form or fashion without the written consent of the author.

Press release kits are available on the website at
www.BooksByElder.com

My name is Francis Elder II and I am an American. I say that with pride because I feel that statement really means something good. The United States of America is known as the "Land of the Free" and the "Land of Opportunity", I whole heartedly believe in those terms of endearment for this wonderful country of ours.

I am going to discuss some of the insights I have made during my almost forty-seven years on this green globe we call Earth. In addition, I am also going to discuss reasons why I and so many other American's have become disenfranchised with American politics.

Am I a political expert? No. Am I part of a lobbying firm? No. What I am is just an ordinary person that has tried to make sense of our political machine for a very long time.

My opinions and suggestions are just that, mine. Having lived for almost five decades I have interacted with many people from all different walks of life, each had their own opinions on the matter, sometimes our opinions corresponded and sometimes they did not.

What I would like to see is more engagement by the "general public" in the governance of our country. Currently, if you ask the average person on the street if they feel that they can actually contribute to how our country is run and the laws that are in place, the larger majority would not show much confidence in their ability to do so.

In this book I am going to touch on many areas that I feel need change and some of these changes are pretty major. I am not someone talking about overthrowing our government but we as the citizens of the United States of America are the ones that have to shape our future as a whole. We have become too dormant in the matters of law and politics.

I hope to engage each of you on a level that is personal to yourself and encourage each of you to become more involved and proactive. The future is ours to shape.

I fully believe that together we can continue to make the United States of America a shinning beckon of freedom and prosperity, continuing the evolution of this great country in a positive way. For those that say we need a "revolution", we have already had one of those. Now is the time of our "evolution". So instead of talking about a revolution let us think and talk in terms of evolution instead. Together we can make this happen.

What I am discussing in this book is primarily how we choose a presidential candidate and making changes so that that choice is actually by the people. Also I am discussing the federal judicial system in relation to how we fill our congress, how we sponsor our bills, how those bills become law and what changes should be made so that the citizens of America are included in the making of laws.

There will be discussion in regards to state and municipal level legislation as well and many of these ideas and principals can be applied universally.

Table of Contents

Introduction   i

CHAPTER 1
America The Beautiful   1,2
The Founding Fathers   3,4,5

CHAPTER 2
2016 Presidential
Election   6,7
The Nastiest
Presidential Election Yet   8,9
Surrogates And The
News   10,11
Disenfranchised Voters   18,19

CHAPTER 3
Professional Politicians   13,14
In It For Themselves   15,16
Partisan Bickering   17
Filibuster   18,19

CHAPTER 4
How Did We Get Here?   20
Voter Turnout   21
Economic Divide   22,23
Riders   24
Accountability   25,26,27
Status Quo   28

CHAPTER 5
Get Out And Vote!   29,30
Resource Availability   31
Voter Offices   32
Internet Voting   33,34
Federal And State
Assistance   35,36

Employer
Responsibilities   37,38
Voter Security   39
Language Barriers   40
Veterans And Active
Service Members   41

CHAPTER 6
Limiting Terms And
Employment   42,43
Term Limits   44
Vote Participation   45
After Their Term   46

CHAPTER 7
Limiting Pay And Perks   47
Pay   48
Special Interest Money
And Gifts   49
Travel And Lodging   50
Yearly Audits   51

CHAPTER 8
Lobbying Changes   52,53
Federal Permits   54
The Fees   55,56
Accountability   57

CHAPTER 9
Two Party System   58,59
Partisan Politics   60
No More   61

CHAPTER 10

Congress   62,63
Come Together   64,65
Representing Each
State   66
Americans Expectations
Of Government   67

CHAPTER 11

Voting Changes   68
Presidential Elections And
The Electoral College   69,70
Getting Elected To
Be President   71,72,73
Voting Schedules   74,75

CHAPTER 12

Making A Law   76,77
Public First   78,79
State Of Emergency   80
State And Municipal
Legislation   81

CHAPTER 13

Removing A Law   82,83
Away It Goes   84

IN SUMMARY

85,86

SPECIAL

ACKNOWLEDGEMENT

87

America The Beautiful

"We must look back and reflect upon our history as there is no wiser teacher or guide to our future." ~F. Elder II

How we shape our future lies with how we lived our past and the lessons we have learned from that past. History does show who we were, but it does not determine who we will be.

It is important that we look at lessons learned from our past and read carefully the details of that history. There is a great saying that goes like this; "Hindsight is 20/20". Which is why I feel it is important to teach our children history, true and untarnished by opinion.

The latter of which is sometimes very hard to take out of the mix. We all form our own opinions about what matters to us and even form opinions on the things that matter little to us. It is very easy to have a closed view once we have formed an opinion about something and therein lies the challenge, keeping an open mind to opposing views.

History for example is a subject of much opinion in regards to the great things that have happened in our past and the horrific things that have happened as well. There are those that would even argue that certain events, good or bad, never took place. No matter how much evidence is provided to the contrary they will still hold steadfast to their beliefs that the event never transpired.

Hiding our heads in the sand will not make those instances in history go away, but owning them will make us better. What do I mean by term "owning them"? I mean we realize what has happened and take responsibility for the good as well as the bad.

We have been given this gift called life. It is up to each of us to decide how we live our lives and whether we learn from our mistakes or just keep repeating them?

History is important, but do not dwell so long in the past that you forget your future.

The Founding Fathers

The prominent thinking in regards to who the "Founding Fathers" were of the United States of America is; John Adams, Benjamin Franklin, Alexander Hamilton, Thomas Jefferson, James Madison, James Monroe and George Washington.

In a much broader spectrum there are others that will say that the Founding Fathers are those who signed the Declaration of Independence, those who helped in the drafting of the Constitution of the United States, delegates to the 1787 Constitutional Convention, those who signed the Articles of Confederation and the signers of the Continental Association.

My theory on the matter is even broader. To me personally I feel that the "Founding Fathers and Mothers" were everyone that fought for our independence, they are our true founders. Let me be clear on this point, I do not mean just those that took up arms in the name of independence, but all who helped support that notion of a free and independent country.

I believe that those who signed the Declaration of Independence sought not only our freedom from oppression but to frame the beginnings of a country that put individual freedoms and the ability for individual prosperity at the head of the table.

This was to be our new beginning and the ability for us as a people to guide ourselves in a fair and just manner. To end a time of oppression and stop those that would insist on having us live by their rule of law.

Now with that said, there is a key passage in the Declaration of Independence that I can not agree with and in my opinion was a very two faced statement to make in this very important document.

"He has excited domestic insurrections amongst us, and has endeavoured to bring on the inhabitants of our frontiers, the merciless Indian Savages whose known rule of warfare, is an undistinguished destruction of all ages, sexes and conditions."

Our country was founded by murdering and relocating a people that were here before we were and had every right to live in a country with the same protections as those afforded every citizen of the United States of America.

Some people do not realize that there was a passage that was written by Thomas Jefferson that followed the above quoted passage, that passage is as follows;

"He has waged cruel war against human nature itself, violating its most sacred rights of life and liberty in the persons of a distant people who never offended him, captivating and carrying them into slavery in another hemisphere, or to incur miserable death in their transportation thither. This piratical warfare, the opprobrium of infidel powers, is the warfare of the Christian king of Great Britain. Determined to keep open a market where MEN should be bought and sold, he has prostituted his negative for suppressing every legislative attempt to prohibit or to restrain this execrable commerce: and that this assemblage of horrors might want no fact of distinguished die, he is now exciting those very people to rise in arms among us, and to purchase that liberty of which he has deprived them, by murdering the people upon whom he also obtruded them; thus paying off former crimes committed against the liberties of one people, with crimes which he urges them to commit against the lives of another."

This was in my opinion his declaration of distaste for the practice of slavery even though he himself owned slaves. But that passage was stricken from the declaration by Congress, acquiescing to the desires of South Carolina and Georgia who desired to continue the slave trade.

Were the founding fathers perfect? Did they do all the right things all of the time? The answer is no. But in the larger scheme of things their intentions were to help create a country that promoted prosperity, a fair rule of law and the application of that law.

2016 Presidential Election

"Loyalty to country ALWAYS. Loyalty to government, when it deserves it." ~ Mark Twain

Confidence. Noun. full trust; belief in the powers, trustworthiness, or reliability of a person or thing. That is the text book definition of a word that means so much to each and every one of us. I have to tell you something and I know many of you are in the same boat as I am, I have little to no confidence in those running for the presidency of the United States of America this election.

Voter confidence is at an all time low and yet with this being the case it is still just "business as usual" for those already elected to serve our needs. For the candidates, every day represents a new chance to fling mud and spew hatred towards one another in an attempt to sway the voters to their side, one could say it is business as usual for the candidates as well.

This has to be one of, if not the worst elections in the history of our country. So many Americans are disheartened by the antics of these candidates to a point that it really is depressing. I could envision a new malady that comes out of this election, requiring insurance companies to scramble and identify how this will be classified and the appropriate payout limits.

Post Presidential Election Disorder (PPED). In a world filled with trending topics and hash-tags the one hash-tag I hope not see is #PPED. Yes, I am being a tad facetious and am well aware of that fact. But can you really say with "confidence" that this really may not become a thing?

The Nastiest Presidential Election Yet

I have seen a lot of bitter and downright "hit below the belt" elections in my life. There have been plenty of examples of shenanigans through out the history of our country in relation to presidential elections as well as other elections held on the federal, state and local levels.

But personally I have to say this tops any that I have seen and disgusts me to my core. I have heard those same sentiments from so many others, people just like me who dread turning on the news or reading a newspaper, because we are going to be inundated with these foolish antics.

How can you expect the American public to have faith in our system when those that say they are the most capable to run our country act like school children on a play yard, fighting over the monkey bars.

We talk about bullying in our society and in our schools and how we have to stop it dead in its tracks. We expect our children and our fellow adults to treat each other in a certain way, to not bully and degrade others, just because that is how bullies get to feel better about themselves.

As a society we have put our foot down on the practice of bullying and we have rising with a unified voice saying that it is not acceptable in this day and age.

Yet here we have candidates acting in that same fashion and somehow that is supposed to be alright in this case? Is the message they are trying to send one that states it is alright to act like this because it involves something so very important? That seems to be the case and it could not be further from the truth.

These people, these individuals that want our vote, they are supposed to be the example of the best of our country, because we are supposed to believe they care about all citizens the same and want what is best for everyone.

Their actions speak opposite to that sentiment. Their actions have done nothing to prove to us they are "presidential material". The leader of the most powerful country in the world, the shining beckon of freedom and prosperity, is supposed to exude a certain decorum. Instill a sense of trust in those they serve, the citizens of the United States of America.

But this has not been the case so far and with precious few days left in the campaign process my hope, the hope of many others, is fading quickly.

Surrogates And The News

I have seen this trend towards news channels in using political surrogates for "reporting" and I can not believe that this is allowed to happen. I know we have a long history of news reporting agencies taking sides for one candidate or another and somehow they want us to believe they a proffering to us an unbiased opinion.

A news reporting outlet should be impartial and stating the facts, not using their power and reach to affect the decisions of the masses. But the fact of the matter is that this has happened very often in the past, it is currently happening and it will continue to happen.

How can we combat this issue? With knowledge. Knowledge is power and when that knowledge is given to the people they then have the power to make educated decisions about the issues that matter most to them.

Many people, if not the majority of those who vote, rely on what they see and hear from news reporting agencies to help them decide if a politician is worth voting for or a certain bill is worth passing. With the news outlets being so one sided at times, how can we assure that people are getting the actual facts? By offering more resources on a much larger scale that is how.

We pour billions and trillions of dollars into our military machine to help assure our borders are safe and we can enjoy our way of life. I believe that the election of our officials and the passing of our laws require the same level of commitment and priority.

I am not advocating the level of spending for this as we do our military defenses, but with that said there is much waste in the government that could be trimmed and used elsewhere for the betterment of our citizens. I will discuss further into this book my ideas on how we can help accomplish this particular goal, perhaps without even having to tap into other services budgets.

Disenfranchised Voters

So many of us dread watching the news during election years, full well knowing that our senses are going to be bombarded with the vilest of mud slinging, innuendos and hypocrisy. The same can be said for print news, online news, social media and other non-traditional forms of communication.

This continual bombardment of crap, for lack of a better word, not only disenfranchises voters but also desensitizes them to an event that should hold great importance to each and every one of us, the selection of the president of the United States of America.

If a presidential candidate has to resort to anything other than the facts are they really the person we want representing this great country of ours to the rest of the world? Are they the person we can entrust with our future and the future of our children and their children?

Personally I feel more people will participate in our voting system if they feel they are actual stake holders in their futures and that their votes not only matter but can actually make a difference for the good of our country.

How are we going to get to that place from where we are now? By bringing confidence back to the people that their government is a government "By The People, For The People". We need to remind these politicians that take us for granted, that they work for us, The People.

Professional Politicians

"Politics is the art of looking for trouble, finding it everywhere,
diagnosing it incorrectly and applying the wrong remedies."
~ Groucho Marx

Whyat is a "Professional Politician" you ask? It is a term I tend to use for those politicians that seem to be in it not for being a public servant but for the pay during and after their tenure, the power, the perks, the benefits and basically just what they can get out of the position.

I think so many of today's politicians, especially those older and more entrenched politicians, have lost track of what it means to be a public servant. Perhaps they really never had an understanding of that concept in the first place, I think that also holds true in many instances.

To me a public servant is someone that goes to work on a daily basis with a sense of concern, more specifically a sense of concern for their fellow human beings, which happen to be those that have elected them and rely on them to always look out for their best interest.

Hopefully at the end of their workday that same public servant goes home with a sense of accomplishment, because he or she has gotten closer that day to creating a positive outcome in regards to those issues of concern.

A small business owner is rewarded by the hard work that they put fourth, showing up each day with a positive outlook and a desire to overcome the obstacles put in front of them. Many times their "pay" is tied into the effort that they put fourth, their livelihood and ability to care for themselves and their families are directly tied into them being proactive and accountable.

But in the realm of the professional politician that kind of concept does not apply. They still get paid even if they do not show up for work and cast votes, they still have a very cushy salary, they still have their medical benefits and they even still have their job.

In the business world if you do not show up to do your work you normally do not get paid and if you do it enough times you lose your job, your benefits and your ability to provide for yourself and your loved ones.

Where is the same accountability for professional politicians? There really is none. Sure, you can say that at the end of their term they can have a replacement voted into the seat they held. But is that really fair? I do not think so and I know a lot of other people that feel the exact same way.

It is time for accountability on a level these professional politicians are not used to having, it is time for some change.

In It For Themselves

I think that there is a lot to be said for a career civil servant, someone who goes to work day after day trying to make a better life for those around them. Striving to make at least that one big significant change that helps the larger majority, all the while looking for those little wins each and every day, knowing that those too will help the masses accumulatively.

But now we get back to the lack of confidence in our professional politicians. Who can blame us? When we are inundated almost day after day with examples of those that are just in it for themselves.

Did you know that Benjamin Franklin, during the Constitutional Convention, actually tried to propose that there would be no pay for elected government officials? It is true! This never happened because the other founding fathers decided otherwise.

There is a lot of incorrect information out there in regards to congressional salaries, their benefits and pensions. I think a lot of that is due to the immense distrust the American public has in our politicians.

The wonderful thing about this day and age is that this information is as close as tapping a few buttons on a keyboard or screen, but that is a double edged sword. There is also a lot of incorrect information out there as well and there needs to be better and more transparent resources available for those that have these kinds of questions.

Personally I feel that the larger majority of politicians out there are in it for themselves and to position themselves into cushy, high paying jobs after their terms are over. I am not the only one that feels this way.

How many of these politicians take advantage of the perks and gifts afforded to them by special interest entities while in office? How many find themselves receiving lucrative jobs after their terms as advisors to lobbying firms or other firms and companies that have benefited from their association with that politician? How many of these people have used the power of their office to benefit themselves monetarily or otherwise?

We The People have lost faith in them and their ability to put us ahead of their own personal needs and aspirations.

Partisan Bickering

When we elected these officials into office it was with the hope and belief that they would be able to work together to fix legislation that was broken and enact new legislation that will help us flourish and provide for our loved ones.

Instead of seeing our hopes come to fruition we instead are inundated with politicians that can see no further ahead than the tips of their noses and seem to care less about putting the peoples needs ahead of their own petty desires.

Our "two party system" may have worked well at one time but that can no longer be said to be true. I can not for the life of me believe that the founders of this great nation had this in mind. I believe if they saw what our government has come to they would be more than just saddened and disappointed, they would be livid.

There is nothing more infuriating than seeing an actual good piece of legislation get trampled on by a bunch of people that seem to have nothing better to do than argue with each other.

If they can not come together with mutual respect and with an earnest desire to serve the people, how in the world can they expect the people to believe they care?

Filibuster

What a great idea! Let us allow tactics that force a decision against the will of the majority and just outright prevents the adoption of a measure that is favored by the majority. Seems logical right? I and many others do not think so.

This inane practice found its roots back in 1806 but it wasn't until 1937 it was used and many say the real defining moment came in 1841, when senator William King threatened a filibuster after senator Henry Clay tried to end the debate on a bill to charter the Second Bank of the United States. King, with the support of other senators, forced Clay to reverse course and finally acquiesce.

This is a great example of people who are expected to serve our needs, doing nothing in essence and to be honest that infuriates me and many others to the core. If you work for an employer and that employer says "We need to come to a consensus on what we are doing on this project, I would like to give each of you a chance to express your thoughts." and then someone who does not agree with the merits of the project decided that he or she would stop all progress for the next several hours or even day by talking the subject to death, what do you think would happen to that employee? I imagine they would be fired.

Yet we allow this to happen on a regular basis, we allow these people that we elected to turn our government into an elementary playground where the bullies want to run the show. This has to change.

The longest debate in US history came from senator Strom Thurmond of South Carolina who was opposed to the Civil Rights Act of 1957. He actually spoke for 24 hours and 18 minutes, this was his attempt to derail this legislation.

If you think that was bad enough there were then teams of senators that continued filibustering for 57 days. From March 26th to June 19th they did their best to keep this legislation from passing, but it was finally passed on that last day.

This is just one example, but such an important example. The Civil Rights Act of 1957 was undeniably important and needed, it was the right thing to do and should have been done sooner.

Instead of embracing such a positive piece of legislation these professional politicians decided to do their best to derail it instead, using any method they could.

This happens too often and many times because someone has their own vested interest. Perhaps they have a government contract for military hardware in their state, or an oil company is in their back pocket or other special interests promising them monetary gain.

We need to remove the filibuster option, this is an outdated tactic that does far more harm that it does good. Honestly, are we going to continue to allow a 200 year old practice hold us hostage?

How Did We Get Here?

*" All of us who are concerned for peace and triumph of reason
and justice must be keenly aware how small an influence reason
and honest good will exert upon events in the political field."*
~ Albert Einstein

Voter turn out for presidential elections dropped right around 5% in 2012 compared to 2008. It was even lower than 2004 by nearly 2%, but higher than voter turn out in 2000 by about 8%. What do all these numbers mean? That during the last two elections voter turnout has continually dropped.

Americans have gotten so frustrated and disenfranchised with our political system that many have opted to just not participate in one of the most important processes in our country. They have gotten such a bad taste in their mouths for "politics as usual" that to them they would rather not choose between the better of two evils.

We as a people have allowed the system to get where it is today and there is no button to push that will make it better, it just does not work that way. Burying our heads in the sand is what has gotten us to this point and it is time to pull our heads out, shake off the sand and start making things happen that need to happen.

Voter Turnout

I mentioned earlier the percentages of decrease in voter turn out that has been occurring over the past two presidential elections. Numbers I have seen floating around put us at somewhere around 200 million registered voters for the upcoming 2016 election.

If we continue on the trend that we have seen over the past two elections that means we could see a lack of voter turn out somewhere around the 8% mark. That may seem like a low number but that is pretty darn close to 1/10th of the registered voters.

Assuming that we have around that 200 million registered voters for 2016, if we have a lack of voter turn out of around 8%, that represents 16 million voters basically saying that it is not worth their time or effort to help make this huge decision for our country.

We have to engage these voters and encourage them to get out and vote and be proactive in their government, at all levels. Right now though that is an uphill battle due to the lack of confidence that Americans have in our political system. I have said it before and I will say it again, something has to change.

Economic Divide

I strongly believe that voter turnout is affected directly by the huge economic divide our country is seeing. So much has been discussed on the topic of the ever shrinking middle class, how it affects our economy, our schools, medical care, education opportunities and so on.

I feel that there is also a direct correlation between the increasing economic divide between what we have termed as the "have and have-nots" to the level of activity in relation to voter turnout.

Let us take for example single parents and the struggles they go through to provide for their family. I have seen various numbers quoted that put the numbers to somewhere around 14 million single parents, men and women combined.

To provide for their children they work not only a full time job a large part of the time but in many instances they end up with a second job. They put in a tremendous amounts of time and energy to just provide the basics for their children, let alone start saving for things like college.

This has created a part of our society that is working so hard to provide for their families that they have very little time for anything else. Being with their kids takes up so much of the rest of their free time, as it should, it leaves almost no free time.

With all this time spent, do you really think they put as a priority trying to stay up on how their representatives in congress are doing in relation to their needs? Do they feel they have enough time to research what laws are coming up and if they agree or disagree with what is being proposed? Are they going to take time to really research a candidate when they have such a preciously small amount of time left in their day? No is the most likely of answers.

The minimum wage has not kept up with inflation, that is a fact. The percentages are what get disputed and argued to the Nth degree. Personally I think that the minimum wage should increase to no less than $14 per hour and that is a number my "gut" tells me is right. So maybe that number is right and maybe it is not, but the fact remains that it needs to be substantially raised.

I think most Americas, when asked, would say that they feel our government has not done enough to keep jobs in our country. Take for example manufacturing jobs, something that this countries middle class has been built upon. Since 2000 we have lost somewhere in the neighborhood of 5 million of these jobs. No one in their right mind can say this has not adversely affected us.

Yes, there may very well be a shift in the job market towards more "tech" industries, but that does not mean there is a lack of need for jobs in manufacturing. We have just allowed them to taken out from under us.

Riders

This is another area that just chaps my hide to no end and is a practice that just should not happen. Legislatures' may tell you that this is sometimes the only way to get some laws passed that need to be passed, but that is a crock. The practice of using riders exists at the federal level as well as the state level.

What is a rider? A rider is an additional provision that gets tacked onto a bill or other measure. The legislature then has to consider it along with the primary bill or measure. Many of the times these riders never have anything to do with the bill or measure they are put upon.

So many times a rider is an item that on its own would not be able to stand up to a vote so instead some sneaky politician decides to try and weasel it into law. I know it is out there in plain sight and can be reviewed by all, so technically it is not being snuck into anything. But that is what I call it when you have to attach a controversial provision that would not pass on its own.

We have allowed this tactic to be used for far too long and at the end of the day it rests at our feet that this practice happens.

We need to remove this practice immediately. This tactic is a primary example of a tool that is used to pass useless provisions with limited benefits but to a select few. In addition, the use of riders have also helped contribute to how bloated our legal system has become.

There are so many laws that are just not needed, that are outdated and should be removed. But this practice allows even more laws that hold little value to the general populace of America to be implemented.

Accountability

We really do not hold our lawmakers accountable at the end of the day for the majority of their actions. The only time there is a big deal made about something, seems to be when it gains a lot of media attention.

Once that pot has gotten stirred then we see lawmakers become proactive and Americans have little faith in the outcome of such activities. How many times does it seem that various lawmakers become proactive just because they want some face time on the television? It seems that they want to use those moments to "remind us" why we voted them in. Here they are being proactive, showing that they can be tough and hold others accountable. What a great way to remind us of their importance.

Then once the "issue" has died off they go back to business as usual and what has the outcome been of this public showing? Generally not a lot. How many times have we seen congressional hearings where those that are called before congress to testify either just do not show up, or they refuse to answer any questions under the 5th amendment? Too many!

If we are going to allow these types of hearings then we had better put some teeth in them, otherwise all they are is a waste of taxpayer dollars and time. Time that could have been better spent addressing health, education, employment issues and so on. If a witness is called to testify before congress and they do not show up, there needs to be consequences that are real and actionable. If a witness refuses to answer questions the same should apply.

Voting is another area that really chaps my rear, in regards to the lack of voting by those we have elected to represent our needs. They work for me and they work for you. Yet, they feel it is ok to miss votes and just not take the time to show up and represent their constituents.

Another thing that really ruffles my feathers is when a lawmaker decides to abstain from voting. He or she is there physically but feel so indifferent about what is coming up for a vote that they decide to just abstain and not vote at all. We the people did not put you in your position to be undecided, we put you in this position because you convinced us you were the right choice to assure our best interests are met.

If these people were in the regular job market and treated their obligations to their employer the same way, what would happen? Most likely they would get fired and that is what needs to happen. If you do not participate in a certain amount of votes, lets say for example 85% of all votes that come before you in a year, you do not have a job the next year. Then we find someone else to take your place. End of pay, end of benefits, end of employment.

I think that kind of percentage would be fair. That would allow for those few times that they may be too sick to make it in for work or they have a family emergency or some other emergency that really required their attention, versus the voting process.

Status Quo

Simple put, we have allowed a status quo that does little to incentivize our lawmakers to put in 100% effort after we have voted them into office.

When the status quo stays the same why should we expect any sort of a different outcome months and years down the road? We really can not, that is the answer. So we have to change the status quo and light a fire under the butts of these professional politicians and remind them that they work for us and that we will hold them accountable.

Chapter

5

Get Out And Vote!

*" I predict future happiness for Americans, if they can prevent
the government from wasting the labors of the people under the
pretense of taking care of them." ~ Thomas Jefferson*

There really is only one way to assure that our government does what we the American people want it to do and that is to be proactive. We are the ones that have to hold our government officials accountable to assure that they maintain the highest standards and rise to our expectations.

We can grumble and complain as much as we want but at the end of the day it is about each and every one of us standing up to be heard and never taking no for an answer. If we come together as one we can accomplish any task and achieve any goal. But it takes a united front and a united voice to be heard.

One very effective way to be heard and assure our best interests are at the forefront is to vote. I will be honest and say there have been times in the past that I have chosen not to vote because for me it was the principal of refusing to vote for the lesser of two evils.

In hindsight I think that was wrong and did very little to almost nothing to help the situation during those times. As I have grown older and lived life my opinions have changed in many areas including politics.

We have to be proactive! Even if that means penciling in your choice after much consideration. I am even ok with penciling in your favorite cartoon character. Why? Well just imagine if in 2012 a large percentage of those who did not vote actually voted in for a fictional character. Votes are tracked and accounted for and I guarantee you that if 5 or 10 million votes were cast for various fictional characters that would have made headlines.

So instead of just being quiet and not voting at all, you have spoken up to show your disappointment in the status quo and speaking out in any form means something.

Within this book are going to be numerous changes proposed that I feel will help better educate our citizens, so that they can actually make better and more informed decisions on who they are going to vote for and the laws that are going to be passed.

I do not profess to have all the answers or have the ability to just flip a switch and make it better for everyone. I am though willing to put my ideas out there, show my disgust for the status quo and do my best to try and help change what needs to be changed.

At the end of the day though it is all about being proactive. So if you have better ideas, different ideas, you need to make your voice heard and you need to be proactive.

The other really important thing? You need to vote!

Resource Availability

In this day and age there really is no reason for not having better resources available for voters to research candidates that are up for election, current members of congress, proposed laws and the current laws that govern our country on the federal, state and municipal levels.

The average citizen of the United States of America should be able to, with very little outside guidance, research all of the above mentioned areas. In other words, this information needs to be made more transparent and easier to access.

In addition, the act of being able to place votes needs to be made more accessible to all voters. We have dealt for far too long with inequity in relation to the ability for all citizens to easily, with as little disruption in their lives as possible, be able to cast their votes for federal, state and municipal laws.

Once the level of resources are adequate we will see more participation by our citizens in a much broader spectrum, I fully believe that to be a true statement. With that increased participation will come a greater feeling of ownership by our citizens in regards to how we are governed.

This will also lead to greater accountability for those we elect to govern and a much more effective means by which to affect change when change is required.

Voter Offices

For far too long we have relied on setting up many temporary voter facilities during the voting process, hoping that there will be enough of these facilities set up around the country to accommodate those wanting to vote in all the areas needed.

What we need are permanent stand alone voting offices in a quantity sufficient to allow every American the opportunity to vote, this could also be augmented with mobile voting offices that can travel into places such as very rural areas, rehabilitation facilities and care centers where those that are not mobile can be assured a way to cast their vote that is easy and convenient to them.

The permanent voting offices can also serve the dual purpose of information depots. Where any citizen can go to utilize an efficient and standardized system which will allow them to research candidates, current lawmakers, current law and proposed legislation on the federal, state and municipal level.

In addition to the permanent stand alone voting offices we should setup every library that receives state or federal funds with their own "in house" voting/research areas that utilize the same technologies that will be employed in the stand alone offices.

Yes, this may mean that some if not most libraries will require renovations, some to a small degree and others to a much larger degree, to accommodate these areas. This will not only help assure that there are more than adequate resources for voters but it will also help the economy in so far as creating jobs to do these renovations, with emphasis given on trying to utilize as much "local" labor as possible. The jobs produced in this type of infrastructure upgrade will run across a broad spectrum of professions; masonry workers, carpenters, painters, plumbers, electricians, IT professionals and so on.

Internet Voting

Our society is growing by leaps and bounds, not only in volume of people but also in regards to the propagation of technology. That technology is making our lives easier and more productive day by day.

We need to embrace technology and work on ways to integrate technology into our voting process more. There will be those that ring the bell of alarm about fears of hacking, voter manipulation and so on. This is not a new issue we have dealt with, it has reared its ugly head for a very long time. In fact, we hear accusations of voter manipulation even during this upcoming presidential election.

I personally feel that the more we can utilize technology and show that it is safe and secure to utilize in the voting process, the greater the level of interaction we will have with our citizens. We will have much higher voter turnout and participation.

Is this something that can happen tomorrow? To be honest I am not sure how quickly it can be rolled out, but what I do feel is that we need to switch some gears and put more effort into making this a reality and to make this happen sooner than later.

Our societies view on the utilization of technology is much more accepting now than it was say 25 years ago and that is due in part to the proliferation of technology today compared to that period 25 years ago.

With change comes push back, that is inevitable. Just because there is resistance to change does not mean that the change should not occur and is not for the betterment of our citizens and society as a whole. This is an area we need to explore now and with greater effort.

I would foresee the utilization of digital balloting in all of the "voter offices", as the logistics of utilizing old fashioned paper ballets just is not realistic in the broader future picture. If implemented properly I could also see this as a way of assuring voter manipulation is not occurring.

This form of voting would really help those that are disabled, traveling or by some other reason unable to get to a voter office.

Federal And State Assistance

Simply put, if you as a citizen of the United States of America and receive any sort of federal or state assistance, you must participate in the voting process. Otherwise you risk loosing whatever benefits you are receiving. In the case of something like social security, you would be removed from the ability to participate in that program. Perhaps a clause is put in place where if this happens the participant only gets back a percentage of what they have paid into social security, thus incentivizing further the participation in the voting process.

This may sound cold hearted at best and near impossible at worst, but I fully believe that it is not only our right as United States citizens to be able to participate in the voting process but it is also our duty to help ensure a free and democratic country. Unfortunately as harsh as this may sound I really feel it is needed.

If we have in place the resources that allow our citizens to vote such as the voting offices, mobile voting offices, the ability to cast a vote online etc... then there should be no reason for those that receive assistance through federal and state programs that would keep them from playing their part in our voting system.

Much like how the requirement for those in congress to participate in a certain percentage of votes, to keep their jobs, there should also be a similar requirement of those that receive assistance from federal and state programs to keep those benefits.

I would see a requirement for each of them to participate in the election of a president, unless there is a medical reason or state of emergency that keeps them from being able to fulfill those duties.

In regards to all other votes that they can participate in on the federal, state and municipal levels, there should be say for instance a 75% requirement, also with the only exceptions being medical or a state of emergency.

If those requirements are not met then they are removed from whatever programs of assistance that they are on.

Certain provisions would need to be put in place for service members during deployment, especially if during a state of war, but I would imagine that even in a large part of those instances they should still be able to vote with some needed changes taking place, this would of course apply to certain family members of those service members.

I would think that there should be some sort of provision that allows those that have been removed from various benefits due to a lack of participation in the voting process, to be able to regain those benefits in some way. Perhaps by participating the following year the required amount will allow them back into the programs starting the proceeding year and from then on, unless they fail to meet the requirements again.

Employer Responsibilities

Employers must give time off to every eligible employee for them to be able to vote, with some changes I will discuss further into the book employees will be able to schedule this time off so that it does not adversely impact their employer.

Each employer can offer a per diem to their employees for going to vote, helping to encourage them to get out and vote. This per diem could be up to a certain amount, lets say for instance $35. The employer would not be responsible for paying the employee a wage for the time spent away from work to go vote if that employee is an hourly wage earner.

The employer could then take a tax credit for the exact amount that they pay the employee as a per diem payment for going and voting. Yes the employer may lose some time in relation to production by that employee but they gain a valuable tax credit that can help them with their tax burden and it is the right thing to do.

An employer can not dock any employee in any way for going to vote, either through pay, point systems or promotion and advancement opportunities.

Some may look at this and say that it would be abused by employees who would instead just take time to go home or just do other things during that time frame that do not pertain to the voting process.

That is always a chance, but a limited one I think. Remember there will be certain rules effecting a percentage of voters who currently receive federal or state assistances if they fail to meet certain guidelines for voting. In addition, there will be the provision in regards to benefits such as social security, which effects a large portion of our citizens.

The only people that that would really be able to take advantage of this in that way would be those that receive no federal or state assistance and have their own retirement plans set up where they will not have to rely on social security.

With that all said I think that our citizens should be able to decide on weather they pay into programs such as social security or not. If they choose to never pay into that program, they can never receive those benefits. If they choose to only pay certain amounts during certain periods of time that will change their benefit amount once they are able to utilize that program.

Voter Security

I have talked about utilizing technology more in our voting process and am a firm believer that we need to embrace the use of technology in that process.

Probably for as long as there has been a voting process there have been those that have alleged voter fraud and manipulation. Even with putting into place new systems that in reality wind up being more secure, those allegations will still be made.

If we go to a digital format for voting we can utilize various technologies to help assure that the process is secure, as secure and most likely more secure than the system we have in place now.

We can utilize technologies such as biometrics, where the voter identifies themselves by not only showing their voter ID card but then scan a finger print, a palm print or perhaps an iris scan. There are numerous options available.

I see this as a way to increase voter security as well as help streamline the voting process and enable those that are far away from home to cast their votes in not only federal related matters but also for the closer to home state and municipal votes as well.

Anytime you can remove a "paper trail" and the associated labor involved to manage that paper trail, you will save money. Utilizing technology in the voting process is going to happen, it really is not a matter of when but how soon. Why should we continue to procrastinate when the technology is available now?

Language Barriers

Language barriers can not be the reason why someone does not participate in the voting process. If you are a citizen of the United States of America you need to participate in the voting process and in some cases will be required to, so that you may retain certain benefits.

I have no issue in continuing to offer the information pertaining to and for the process of voting in multiple languages in the fashion we provide it currently. The way this happens does need to change.

Another advantage of using technology in the voting process is that we are able to either use current translation software or are at the precipice of being able to use this type of translation software. This software is so much more accurate than it ever has been and to a point that it should be reliable enough to use now.

Imagine someone that is a citizen of the United States of America that may have issues in understanding the English language comfortably and that can now research candidates, bills, laws and be able to vote easier. All because they can now with the click of a button translate that information into their native tongue.

I do feel though that part of citizenship must be the requirement to learn the basic fundamentals of the English language, as that is the primary language we have adopted and utilize in our country. It is a current requirement of the naturalization process and needs to remain, so I am not suggesting any changes to that at all.

Veterans And Active Service Members

Right now those active military service members and overseas voters must request an absentee ballot, sometimes this may include eligible family members as well. We tell every citizen in the United States of America that their vote counts, yet we make our service members jump through more hoops than others to be able and vote.

By using technology we can avoid this issue all together and they can cast their vote on base just like every other American. In fact they should probably be allowed to start their voting earlier just because there are so many variables in regards to their active deployment. Still allowing the use of absentee ballots if there is the rare occasion that they are required.

Every military base in our country should have voting stations and that applies to every military base we have abroad as well. Those that are operating out of a Forward Operating Base should also be able to cast votes when possible. Many people do not realize just how difficult it is for our active duty service members to cast a vote.

In regards to our veterans, there are programs that help transport them to polling stations but those programs need to be increased. By utilizing technology this will immediately help with the issue but we need to still do more. Every veterans hospital, rehabilitation center or other government structure that houses any veteran for a prolonged period of time needs to have a voting office located within it so that veterans can easily and readily cast their votes.

Limiting Terms And Employment

*"Just because you do not take an interest in politics does not
mean politics will not take an interest in you." ~ Pericles*

D isgust. This word can be used by many of our citizens when
looking at what our politicians have accomplished over their
tenure. Some of those tenures have gone on for decades
allowing certain negative mindsets to be entrenched into our
government.

Take for example issues involving race. How long did this country
battle itself in an effort to change something that should never have
been an issue to start with? Far too long is the answer.

How many of these "old" politicians, that have been in place for far
too long, fought the changes that were being proposed in regards to
race related issues? Far too many is the answer.

When we allow old, outdated, negative thought processes to linger
in our government it is almost like allowing a loaf of bread to sit in a
breadbox for a month. Then we open that bread box and take a
good close look at the loaf of bread inside and we find something
that disgusts us, makes us sick to our stomach and repulses us to our
core.

Our government must be fresh and current to be useful and effective in our current and future society. That does not happen when you have people stuck in old out dated modes of thinking at the helm. Yes there is wisdom and knowledge that comes from time but there is also apathy and a feeling that the status quo is alright, this can not be acceptable anymore.

Term Limits

I, as well as many others out there, am a firm believer in setting strict term limits. By setting term limits we emphasize to and remind those we have voted into government that they must make every day count. They must work hard each and every day they are in office to do the best that they can for those they serve, the American People.

There should be only one term for all of those who serve in our legislature and that should be a 4 year term with the opportunity to run for one additional term. That additional term can be consecutive if they win re-election or they can run at a later date. But they are limited to a total of 8 years maximum.

If we do shorter term limits, that will hinder progress and if we allow long term limits along with the ability to be re-elected indefinitely we get stuck in the rut we are now, so we have to find a better solution.

In the case of a member of congress that has been removed from office due to dereliction of duty, a criminal matter or any other reason other than say for instance due to a medical issue, they can no longer run for congress.

If the reason for their removal from office is due to a medical reason, they may only run for office if an opening is available and are bound by the same term limits. So for example if they had to be removed due to a medical issue and were out of office for several months, but the medical issue was resolved and they were fit to continue, they could run in the special election that had been convened to fill the vacant spot. But they must be re-elected for the remainder of their term and convince the voters they are the right person to continue the job.

Vote Participation

Each member of congress must vote in an average of 85% or more of the votes available to them during the course of a year. If they fail to meet this minimum percentage average they will be fired from their position.

There will be no abstaining from a vote, ever. They must vote yes or no, which means they must participate to the fullest extent to meet the expectations of the citizens of the United States of America, who at the end of the day pay their salaries.

This is very important, because we have too many instances of those who we have elected to represent our needs either not show up for various votes or sometimes abstain from voting while they were present.

That practice is unacceptable and has to stop. We have "hired" these public servants and there is an expectation that they have agreed to fulfill their duties for the pay they receive, which is funded by the taxpayers dollars. The process of voting on legislation is one of the most vital parts of their jobs and they must meet that obligation.

Allowing a percentage that is less than 100% gives them some wiggle room for family emergencies, sick days, vacation days and such.

I believe this is in line with what would be expected of any employee and that if there were an employee that missed more than 15% of their work duties in a year their job would be in jeopardy. Considering the importance of what our legislators are doing, this is more than fair.

After Their Term

A concern of many citizens is the fact that they hear about those members of congress that take on what could be referred to as "cushy" and "lucrative" jobs after their term is over, at companies that have been directly effected by legislation they have helped pass.

The concern of a conflict of interest with these companies, lobbying firms and special interest groups is real. With the unknown being whether that member of congress had his or her decision to support certain legislation swayed by the promise of big money after their term was up.

One could say that there should be a rule that they are never allowed to work for any lobbying firm, special interest group or company where they have had direct contact with. Nor should they be allowed to work for those entities if they have ever voted in a positive fashion on legislation that benefited those entities in anyway. Personally I think that is too broad a statement and stance to take on the matter.

But I do think that there should be some sort of checks and balances where if there is credible reason to believe that something like this has occurred they will be investigated by congress.

Once that investigation is concluded and if they are found to have done the afore mentioned in a blatant way that was planned and executed by the parties involved, they should be prosecuted. What the exact criteria would be, to be honest, I am not sure.

What I do know is that we have to crack down on this issue better. We have to do something to help assure our citizens that this problem is no longer and issue.

Chapter

7

Limiting Pay And Perks

"In the beginning of a change the patriot is a scarce man, and brave, and hated and scorned. When his cause succeeds, the timid join him, for then it costs nothing to be a patriot." ~ *Mark Twain*

Lifetime pay. That is a term you will hear many people use when describing those that work in congress with the assumption that every member of congress gets their full pay after they serve their term and that is not correct. Only senators are eligible after one full term for a pension and that pension will only be a percentage of their normal pay, not their full pay.

That pension will not be able to exceed 80% of their final salary and many times ends up being a much lower percentage as it is prorated based upon total length of service. Realistically that number could even be in the single digits.

The job that they do is a very important one and one that affects us all in one way or another. These are the people we have hired to see to it that we can continue to enjoy our way of life and that our children and their children can do the same.

But I think there do need to be some changes.

Pay

Those that serve in congress and represent the various states should be paid according to how their state is doing, this creates a performance based employment and encourages them to assure that their state is doing as well as possible.

The calculation should be something like double the average wage for their state. That means that if the average wage for their state is $35,000 then their wage would be $70,000.

Instead of a wage that is in the six figures when their average constituent is making near poverty level.

If they would like a raise the following year then they have to make sure that those who work in their state do better and that is for the overall majority. So if they work to only increase high paying jobs in their state, their pay increase they see will be minimal.

They will have to work to make certain that everyone in their state gets paid more if they want to see an increase the next year in their salary. If things start going on a downward spiral in their state they get hit in the pocket book just like everyone else who lives there.

This is pay based on performance, plain and simple.

Special Interest Money And Gifts

The simplest answer to this is that there just is none allowed at all. When we elect these officials we are entrusting them to be the guardians of our futures. We are believing their words when they tell us they are the ones that will make sure things are good for us, our loved ones, our children, our friends and for every person that lives in our state and our country.

When those that we elect are able to receive lavish gifts, donations of money and so on, we can not trust that these gifts and donations are not being offered to sway their opinion for the betterment of the few and not the whole.

Those that represent us must be above reproach and allowing gifts and donations to them or someone close to them can do no good in that respect.

Letting a congressperson fly on a companies private jet to do official business or even for leisure is not acceptable. Offering them trips for themselves and/or family is not acceptable. You get the meaning of what I am saying, these are the practices of the past that erode the confidence of our citizens.

Travel And Lodging

In regards to travel I fully endorse the idea that travel expenses for member of congress and their staff should be taken care of 100% when it is job related. As well as lodging expenses that are incurred for those same members of congress and their staff.

There are going to be extenuating circumstances sometimes where only certain means of travel are available or certain accommodations are available, which may incur more cost than usual. Perhaps there are also security issues to be dealt with as well that add to the expense and limit what is feasible and what is not, these things will happen.

But I am a firm believer that when possible there is no reason that those individuals can not go ahead and fly business class.

In regards to lodging, unless there is a security issue that can not be resolved, there is no reason why they can not stay in accommodations that the average US citizen would utilize.

Yearly Audits

There should be yearly audits of each congresspersons expenditures, this will give confidence to the citizens of the United States of America that their dollars are being spent responsibly. Too many instances in the past of waste and corruption have made us suspicious and rightly so, it is time to win back our confidence.

Some things may not be able to be audited though and that is just a fact of life in dealing with these things. If including information in an audit will divulge top secret information, it will not be able to be included in that audit. That is just something we have to deal with.

With the implementation of these additional checks and balances that have been discussed and are still to be discussed, we the citizens of the United States of America will be more assured and confident that those who represent us are doing so in an honorable fashion. Because the level of transparency will be much greater.

Lobbying Changes

"As government expands, liberty contracts." ~ *Ronald Regan*

E very state has different rules and requirements in regards to the practice of lobbying. Some states charge fees of varying amounts while others charge no fees at all. There are also rules and requirements for federal lobbying practices such as the Lobbying Disclosure Act of 1995.

My issue and I think many Americans also have this issue, is that there still seems to be a plethora of lobbyists and lobbying entities out there that throw around insane amounts of money to assure that laws are put on the books that benefit their clients and laws that burden their clients are changed or removed.

Are there good and well meaning lobbyists and lobbying entities out there? I am sure there are and many of them may have the best of intentions. We have allowed lobbying practices to go unchecked for too long and the fixes we have applied are a mere bandage covering a larger wound.

Far too many times have laws that serve only the best interest of the few been passed due in large part to the absurd amounts of money that has been thrown towards passing those laws.

While at the same time, outdated, archaic and all around ineffectual laws have been allowed to stay on the books for the same reasons, those reasons being large amounts of money.

It is time to rip the bandage off and apply some common sense to heal this wound. Doing this is yet another step in rebuilding confidence that has been lost by the American people.

Federal Permits

Personally I think that all lobbyists and lobbying entities should have to be licensed and be given a permit by the federal government, even if they are planning on only lobbying on a state level.

The reason I say this is that many times laws that are enacted at the state level then set precedence for other states. So these laws that are being passed do have the opportunity and in some cases do result in the changing of similar laws in other states, or the passing of similar laws in those other states.

With the changes I have suggested and am going to suggest, these fees will be used to benefit all states in the United States of America, so hang in there with me on this one a little bit longer.

A side effect of having one entity in charge of permits would be the standardization of rules and requirements that will help assure American citizens that every lobbyist and lobbying entity is being treated the same way from state to state and are being held accountable the same.

When action must be taken because a rule has been broken, the remedy is equal across the board and applied swiftly and efficiently. Time is money and the tax payers of this country are tired of having their money wasted!

The Fees

Lobbyists and lobbying firms sometimes pay no fees to register and perform their services, yet they charge handsome fees to their clients. Those clients are more than willing to pay those fees when they feel that laws can be made or changed that will benefit them.

My take on this is that if you are so vested and willing to spend so much money to create or change laws that affect the well being of the citizens of the United States of America, you should be willing to spend enough that it will ensure that those same citizens are aware of what you are doing and get to be informed of everything, so they can make a knowledgeable decision about what is going to transpire and how it will effect them.

With all of that said I think there should be one standard fee of $500 per year for each lobbyist. What this means is that if the lobbyist works alone, he or she will have to spend $500 per year for the standard fee. But if we are talking about a lobbying firm, then the fee applies to each and every lobbyist they employee. Perhaps those firms make the lobbyist pay for it themselves, that is their prerogative and I really do not care. So for instance, if they have 20 lobbyists working for them that will be a standard fee of $10,000 per year. In addition, each principal of the lobbying firm must register as well and their fee is $5,000 per year.

This is a drop in the bucket compared to what they make from their clients and trust me they will end up recouping these fees from their clients, but I am not actually finished yet.

In addition, for every $1000 that is spent in lobbying, $100 dollars goes into a federal fund. That is right, I am talking about 10% of every dollar spent to lobby goes into this fund. Basically, all dollars spent by the entity to lobby for their interest gets an additional 10% fee tacked on that goes into this federal fund.

This fund will help cover the costs of voter offices, the infrastructure for those offices and staff. This shifts the cost of educating our citizens and providing resources that keep them up to date about the laws that lobbyists are trying to change, enact or remove.

In doing my research into how much money is spent annually on lobbying I have seen some staggering numbers. Just looking at various sectors of industry is shocking, for example in 2015 the pharmaceuticals and health products industry spent in excess of $200,000,000.

Just think what $20,000,000 would do to help accomplish increasing voter turn out, voter education and so on. That example is just one sector.

Accumulatively, when you look at the top 10 industry sectors in 2015, over $1,000,000,000 dollars were spent. Yes, that is trillion.

With that being the case, just think what $100,000,000 would do to increase voter turn out and voter education.

Accountability

With going to a standardized system with a single federal database of all lobbyists and lobbying firms, we will be better positioned to enforce the laws that govern lobbying practices.

If a lobbyist is found to be in violation of any rules the repercussions can be swift. The first time they are found to have violated any rules their permit is revoked for a 6 month period. Their second violation results in a permit revocation that lasts for 1 year. Strike three and their permit is removed permanently with no way to ever be in that industry again.

There are no resets, there are only three strikes and you are out.

If a lobbying firm is found to be in violation of any rules the offending parties have their individual permits removed for a 6 month period. A second violation results in the offending parties and the firms permit being revoked for a 1 year period. Strike three results in the permanent removal of the permit of the offending parties and the principals of the firm and the firm is shut down.

Two Party System

*" Politicians and diapers must be changed often, and for the
same reason." ~ Mark Twain*

Time passes and things change. Change just for the sake of
change is generally not a good idea and creates more issues
than it resolves. One of the biggest things that the passing of
time does show us, is what works and what does not. When we do
not listen to the voice and the advice that history shares with us, we
are destined to continue and make the same mistakes over and over.

I am a firm believer that the founders of our great country did not
originally intend for there to be a two party system, but it happened
and has stuck with us for a very long time. The inception of the
second party system in 1824 was the birth of what we know today as
our two party system.

In 1828 the democratic and republican parties were formed. While
the democratic party remained from that point the republican party
went through some changes. It dissolved and became the Whig
party, a party of what were termed modernizers. The early 1850's
marked the end of the Whig party.

Around that same time period there was the Free Soil Party, akin to their name were their beliefs in various freedoms, including that of the slaves. But it too dissolved into nothingness to be replaced by the republican party, consisting of anti-slavery activists, former Whig party members and Free Soilers.

We have been dealing with a two party system for nearly 200 years, perhaps it worked well in the beginning, judging from how this system performs today though I would hazard a guess that our founders would be sorely disappointed.

Partisan Politics

Our legislature is dominated by this two party system and unfortunately the vast majority of those two parties have lost the faith of a very large part of the citizens of the United States of America, due to their sometimes very childish antics.

The strength of the two party system seems unbreakable and has tentacles that stretch out far and wide, choking off true independence. I do not know many people that can honestly say that an independent has a true chance against the system as it operates now.

How often have we seen this group of individuals that we have elected to represent our needs and secure our futures, break down in some childish tug of war over their parties line? Far too often is the answer.

The partisan politics have to end and we have to move forward to a new way of thinking and a new way of doing business. Our citizens, who are the backbone of our country and the life blood of our way of life, deserve better. We struggle every day to make ends meet, to provide for our families and to try and make our lives a little bit better.

Instead of helping us with our struggles, helping us take care of our families and helping us make a better life for ourselves and those around us, these ineffectual representatives of government would rather bicker back and fourth to prove who is right, even if they are wrong and know they are wrong.

Partisan politics can not be our future, it just does not work. We as a country and a society have to move beyond this tired example of what does not work. We need to come together and work with purpose and determination instead of hate, loathing and one-upmanship.

No More

The two party system is old and broken and allowing the status quo will not solve our issues. We have all heard the pandering and the exclamations by various members of government that they "will come together" and "cross the divide" to make our country stronger and the true land of opportunity for all that it is meant to be.

Soon after these words are spoken, they are forgotten. Then it is back to business as usual and the bickering begins yet again.

If you had a business and a small group of employees would take the majority of their day arguing with each other, resulting in either no results or results that took multitudes longer than they should have, what would you do?

I think the answer is you would warn them maybe, right? Sure, that would give them the chance to change their ways and get back on track. What would you do if they ignored you and just continued to argue with each other? You would most likely fire them.

We need to fire the two party system. It is not working and has proven that it just will not work for our future. Get rid of it completely.

From that point on all those who represent our country are "independents". This means that they have to articulate to the country, those that will elect them, that they have the desire and ability to do the right thing. They can no longer rely on a "party" for guidance or to be the scapegoat when things go wrong.

They have to "own it". The buck stops at their feet and if they are either unwilling or incapable of doing what is right for our country, they will get replaced.

Congress

"Extremes to the right and to the left of any political dispute
are always wrong." ~ Dwight D. Eisenhower

Congress consists of two chambers in the federal government, which is known as bicameral legislature. In a bicameral legislature the representatives of the two chambers are generally elected or selected in another manor, members of both houses in the congress of the United States of America are elected by direct popular vote. Senators are voted on at the state by state level, whereas representatives are elected by voters in a specific congressional district.

This is the way our system works presently and I would love to say that it works and works well, but with our two party system that is in place currently all we get are partisan splits that tend to favor one party or another and their agenda.

This in turn locks us into an issue with majority controls, where whichever party has the control ends up dictating the majority of the votes during the time they are in control. There is little recourse for our citizens once this happens and then we are held hostage to the whims of whichever party has the control.

That is when the partisan politics takes over and progress grinds to a screeching halt. That is when those that represent us in the Senate and those that represent us in the House can no longer function as a cohesive unit.

Come Together

It is time that those we have elected come together and put aside partisan politics and do what is in the best interest of those who elected them. They have proven to be ineffectual within the current system, they have proven a change needs to come.

We need to combine the house and the senate. For so long they have been referred to as "both houses", that infers they are separate. That also infers that they have separate agendas for our country.

Yes I know that each side has their specific duties and responsibilities, that is the way the system is set up and has been for a very long time. But just because something has been done one way for a really long time, does that mean it is the right way at this time? No.

If we abolish the house and the senate and instead just have one congress, that has combined powers, with no partisan lines in place, that is the step in the right direction. This unshackles us from indecision due to partisan politics. This puts everyone on the same level playing field.

Everyone has the same term, the same "conditions of employment" and the same expectations of performance. Most importantly the accountability is the same all across the board.

If someone is called before a congressional committee to testify, no longer do they have the excuse of protecting a party to give reason for not showing up, or refusing to answer the questions of the judicial branch. Because there will no longer be partisan lines in congress, they will have one voice that will rule by the majority.

You may ask how I can say that they will have "one voice" when there will be those that disagree and dissent from others. That is the way it should work, those are our checks and balances. If we have given our citizens the proper tools to elect good and honest people to represent us in congress that will mean the majority opinion is the good opinion.

Mistakes can be made, we are after all human. The great thing is though that we will be able to repair our mistakes faster than ever before to help assure we are on the right path for our country.

Representing Each State

Congress will be made up of 8 representatives for each state. Basically the state will be divided up into 8 equal regions and a representative is chosen for each of those regions.

These congressmen and congresswomen then serve the dual purpose of looking after the needs of their states as well as the federal government.

This will help create cohesion across the board and better serve the needs of the individual states as well as the overall needs of the country.

Each congressperson will be provided with a staff of 10 and an office located in the zone they represent and in Washington D.C. The quantity of staff is arbitrary and may need to be changed. The staff members salaries will be capped, just like the congresspersons. I would imagine it should be in the range of 50% above the average wage for their state. This gives an incentive for the staff members to also do their best for the citizens of their state.

Americans Expectations Of Congress

I know I have mentioned this before but I wanted to reiterate that with the changes I have discussed there will no longer be dead weight in the congress. Those that would take the job just for a paycheck, power and perks, will no longer find the position palatable for just those reasons.

We need true civil servants in our congress, we need people there that will do what we have asked of them which is to safeguard our future, so that the future of our children and their children is bright and full of potential.

If a member of congress does not fulfill their duties, they can be easily removed and replaced. Which is the way it should be. There needs to be a sense of urgency by them to keep their jobs and do their best for America and what it offers.

A prime example of this is something I had mentioned before in the book, participating in the voting process. No longer will they be able to abstain from a vote or just not show up, there will be consequences when this becomes an issue. The must vote in 85% of the votes each year to continue their term of employment the following year.

Our expectations of those we have placed in such great power have to be higher than it has been. The accountability for lack of performance has to be higher than it has been.

If our expectations are mediocre at best, how in the world will the results we receive be anything but mediocre? The answer is that they will not.

Voting Changes

" A primary object should be the education of our youth in the science of government. In a republic, what species of knowledge can be equally important? And what duty more pressing than communicating it to those who are to be the future guardians of the liberties of the country?"
~ George Washington

The citizens of the United States of America need to be engaged, encouraged and enabled to participate at a higher degree in relation to the laws that are passed that govern our great country.

Our citizenry are the true checks and balances to our government, they are the stake holders in the future of America and they are the ones that make this country great and full of opportunity.

To that end we need to change up a few things in regards to the voting process. I have already discussed voting offices and making sure that all citizens of this great country have the tools and resources available to not only make knowledgeable decisions but then be able to cast their votes on those decisions. So let me now discuss some voting changes.

Presidential Elections And The Electoral College

How many times are we told that our vote matters and that it is our civic duty to vote? We hear this a lot, in fact I have even mentioned that concept in this book. I truly believe it is our duty as citizens of the United States of America to get out and vote, to make our voice be heard.

With the current system though that voice is muffled, which is why I am throwing out all these ideas in an attempt to get us to not only start thinking about new and better ways of encouraging our citizens to vote but to help ensure that when they do it actually matters and makes a difference.

The Electoral College is another example of a warn out and ineffective system for expressing the true desires of the citizens of America. This is yet another area that requires change.

There are those that believe the presidential elections are a truly popular vote, where the total number of votes are tallied and that alone decides who our president and vice-president will be and that just is not the case.

After those votes are cast and tallied the Electoral College process takes over. Once tallied the political party, in most instances due to the way the two party system works it will be generally be either a republican or a democratic party, that receives the most votes gets control. What that means is that they choose the electors that end up casting the actual votes for president.

States receive electoral votes based on their congressional representation, population is not a factor, with a minimum of 3 with the way congress is set up currently, 2 senators and a minimum of 1 representative.

What we end up with are 538 electors that hold the future of our citizens in their hands. Theoretically a ticket with a low percentage of the popular vote could win, all they have to do is get the majority of the electoral votes.

This means that at the end of the day as few as 270 people may be the ones truly deciding who wins and who goes home with a stocking full of coal. Unfortunately, that stocking full of coal could wind up going out to every citizen in the United States of America in the form of a choice that is not truly what the majority of the citizens of this great country wanted.

We need to get rid of the electoral college and make it a true popular vote. If we have done our part and put into place the changes we need to, the voter turn out will be huge. A much larger cross section of our country will be represented and actually be empowered to make the choices they want.

Getting Elected To Be President

I think that many if not most of the requirements to run for the presidency of the United States of America are good, I honestly do not think there really needs to be much if any change in relation to those requirements.

But now that we no longer have "parties", each candidate is basically an independent. I think that anyone that meets the requirements set fourth should be able to run to be a candidate.

With the new systems in place that allow voters to research candidates, it will be much easier for them to be able to make that all important decision of who they want to run and represent their needs and concerns.

I think that each state should be able to have 1 individual that they have chosen to run for president. But the individuals who want to be considered have to put the time and effort into getting their message out to people.

It would start with getting signatures, the amount required needs to be determined. I am not talking about just walking around with a clip board and getting folks to sign, because then we would have an overhead of someone having to double check that there are no duplicates, that signatures were valid and so on.

This is where we utilize that technology I have spoken about before. I could imagine a hopeful candidate after having been vetted to assure they meet the requirements, would then be able to log into a special page on their smart phone or tablet. Then they could stump for signatures, working the malls, going door to door, traveling across their state, getting supporters to set up "signature parties" where large groups get together and meet with the perspective candidate and then give them in mass their signatures and maybe even be able to just go online and provide their signature etc...

Whatever identification is set up for people to vote is what would be used to get that "signature". The system keeps track of the signatures and keeps a live tally going on the states website. This way each of the prospective candidates can see their standing as can their supporters. At the end of the time period the top two or four perspective candidates get their "election".

People in the state cast their votes for who they want to represent them, this should be over several days to allow as many voters to participate as possible and have as little impact as possible on employers. The votes are tallied almost instantly with the use of this technology and the person on top is the candidate for that state.

From that point we would go into a period of time where the candidates go from state to state campaigning. Their information, videos of campaigns, debates and such are all available online for people to research as well as at all of the voter stations. Allowing those with limited resources to still access this valuable information.

On a certain date a "national primary" is held and the country as a whole votes on who they want in the primaries. The top 4 choices then move on to the actual election.

Again, after a certain amount of time and campaigning the country comes together to make their final vote. That vote should last 1 week, this will give ample opportunity for every citizen that wants to vote, to have the ability to vote. These votes are not live tallied as they are at the state level, the outcome is only announced at the end of the voting period.

It is this vote that determines who the president and vice-president will be. That is right, there will no longer be running mates. The first choice will become president and the runner up becomes the vice-president.

By doing it this way we assure a broad range of applicants to choose from for this job. This also means that we end up putting the two that have been chosen as most qualified into these ever important positions of power.

Voting Schedules

The final presidential election is of course once per 4 year term. The preliminary steps leading up to that final vote will be spaced out accordingly just prior to that voting date.

Considering there are several steps that start at the state level leading up to the final election, each step must be given an adequate amount of time. Perhaps that is a 1 month period for all of the steps leading up to the final election, with the final election being given a 2 month period of campaigning instead, as this is a very important vote.

In regards to federal and state laws, those will be voted on 4 times per year. With that said there will be some federal laws that have to be voted on by only the congress, matters of the top secret nature. These things are going to happen and Americans have to understand that there will be times this is required. But with the much higher level of transparency and accountability that has come with the various changes, they should have much more confidence that their government is doing the right thing in regards to those matters.

That does not mean there should be no audits done internally, utilizing an independent group of congressmen and congresswomen, there should be such audits done on a regular basis for checks and balances.

There should be a time period where the laws are available, less anything top secret, prior to voting which I would imagine is a 2 month period for each. This will give the voters time to research the proposals and decide their merit. If they can not be made available to the public in that time frame the must wait for the next voting cycle.

Then the public votes on the proposed legislation, taking a 1 week period to cast their votes. This will be further discussed in the next chapter.

Local laws will be voted on also 4 times per year, staggered from the federal and state law votes. A time period of review should be available on these laws as well, giving voters 1 month to review and understand the ramifications of the proposed law.

Making A Law

" In the land of the blind, the one-eyed man is king."
~ *Desiderius Erasmus*

Transparency of the law allows us to study the law, to ascertain its usefulness, to ascertain its detriments and then decide if it is in fact a law we need or want. For far too long we have allowed the process of creating laws to be muddied and usurped by those with their own partisan or personal agendas.

We the citizens of the United States of America need to hold ourselves accountable for allowing this to continue and recognize that we ourselves have to take more control of our future and the destiny of our country.

By allowing ourselves to be so effectively removed from the process of creating laws, we have allowed our country to be mired and bogged down in an overly complicated system. This system is so bloated that there is no way we can say it runs efficiently.

Making a law should be one of the most transparent practices we have, with our citizens having full knowledge of what is being proposed and how it will affect them, their friends and family, their children and their children's children.

Removal of the ability for politicians to tack on riders is a first good step, but ultimately we have to become more involved in our society and our rule of law.

Laws should be harder to make than they are to remove.

Public First

Laws on the federal, state and municipal level need to go before the public first. We also need to allow those in Congress and our citizens the ability to bring fourth new laws for consideration on the federal level, as well as the ability to change a law or remove a law.

The exception to that rule would of course be classified information and that as I have mentioned before is going to happen upon occasion, but if the proper checks and balances are in place and we are putting good people into office, this should be much less of an issue than before.

For a congressperson to propose a law they must get above a 33% vote in favor by their fellow congressmen and congresswomen. That vote should take place within a certain amount of time from when it is officially proposed in its final draft form. Once that the minimum vote is achieved it can go to a public vote.

For the public to propose a law they must utilize a process similar to how they would become a potential candidate. They must garner a certain amount of signatures and once those signatures are obtained then it may move on to a public vote. I would imagine the number of signatures will have much different requirements depending upon if it is for the federal, state or municipal level.

The public vote then happens. If it is a federal law being proposed that means it goes into a national vote, the information is placed in the system so that it may be accessed for a 1 month period prior to the scheduled vote.

If it is on a state law being proposed it will go to a state level vote, the information is also placed in the system so that it may be accessed for a 1 month period prior to the scheduled vote.

When it is in regards to a municipal law it will go into that municipalities system for a vote, the information is placed in the system for a 1 month period so that voters may review the information prior to the scheduled vote.

When votes come up for the public they must be passed by 66% or above to move on to congress, state or the municipality. Once in congress, state or municipal government the proposed laws are available for a 1 month period to review and then will be voted on. They must be passed by 70% or above to become law.

During the government review time the applicable government entity may call up to two times for an internal vote to expedite the final vote. That measure must pass by a margin of 66% or more in favor. This will help take care of times of emergency.

State Of Emergency

The president and governors may declare a state of emergency that allows a specific law to be created for the country and states, specific areas or municipalities, presented and brought up for vote without the normal public review process.

This will allow in extreme situations the government to act fast during times of disaster. These laws must be temporary and have a shelf life of no more than 3 months, for them to be extended a separate vote must be made to do so and each extension may only last a maximum of 3 months.

In addition, anytime a state of emergency is called and any law is then passed there must be an immediate audit of the law and how it will affect the citizens directly impacted by those laws. This audit must be completed within 7 days of the law being passed and made public. This also applies to each extension if there are any.

State And Municipal Legislation

Much of what I have spoken about applies to the federal level. With discussion about state and municipal law making as well.

I do not propose to do away with the states legislative branches all together and I will be the first to say I may not have all of the answers here. I believe there should still be a legislative branch but I believe there has to be changes, just like in congress on the federal level.

Perhaps the voting process once completed by citizens in regards to the state then goes to the legislative branch of that state and follows a similar process as has been outlined previously. The same could be said for municipalities.

I am just an average guy trying to figure this out and do my part to be proactive because I know there needs to be a change. Are the needed changes exactly what I have proposed? Only time will tell, along with the consensus of the citizens of America. Wiser minds may come up with much better ideas, I just hope if they are going to it is sooner than later.

Removing A Law

" I am increasingly persuaded that the earth belongs exclusively to the living and that one generation has no more right to bind another to it's laws and judgments than one independent nation has the right to command another." ~ Thomas Jefferson

It seems so much easier to pass a law right now than it is to remove a law. From what I have seen on the federal level we enacted 115 new public laws in 2015. But when I try to research how many we removed during that same year, actually removed, I can not find any examples.

Even looking for examples of repeal and replace laws I did not come across anything and the same applies for partial repeals. Perhaps they are out there, but I could not find any examples for the time period of 2015.

From what I have seen over the many years it is very hard to get a law amended with a partial repeal, replaced or outright removed. This is one of the reasons our system is so bloated and inefficient.

Our legislators have gotten into the mode of thinking that we have to legislate everything to the Nth degree. Sometimes I wonder if they do this just to keep busy and prove to those that voted them in that they are being proactive and doing work.

I think I speak for many Americans when I say I would rather these politicians take their time and gradually add good laws that help us out, instead of rushing as many laws as possible through the system that do so little to help us, yet hold hostage good bills that will never make it into law because they have a personal or party agenda.

Away It Goes

Once per year there should be allowed the ability to votes on removing or changing laws. I know that may not seem like enough considering how many laws we have in place currently, but it is a start that will give back some control to the citizens of this country and give them a voice to be heard when they are dissatisfied.

I would see the process is very similar to the election process and the process used to bring laws into being.

It starts with a petition of signatures about a specific laws in whole or changes to part of a law. These petitions may be made by any citizen including those elected to serve our government. The amount of signatures required should mirror the amount needed to create a law and also be broken up based on if the law is federal, state or municipal.

Once the required number of signatures are received then the vote goes to the people at the appropriate level. First the information is presented for a 4 month period prior to the vote, at the end of that period the vote is taken. If 66% or more of the voters are in favor of keeping the law it will stay otherwise it will move on in the process.

From there the proposition will be taken up on the appropriate level, federal, state or municipal. Then a vote will be taken by the dully elected representatives of the government at the level that is required with the information being presented for 1 month prior to the vote being cast. If the results of the vote are 60% or more in favor of removing or changing the law, it passes. If it does not pass another vote to remove or change that particular law may not be made for another 2 years, helping to limit abuse of this function.

In Summary

Our system of laws and governance is complicated, which is to be expected. We are one of the largest and most powerful of nations on the planet. But our system has become far too complicated and overburdened in many respects, with too many laws that clog the system. In addition, the whole systems lacks the level of transparency that our citizens demand.

I am not a professor of politics, nor am I military tactician or an economic guru. I do not profess to have all or even a large majority of the answers, I just know our system needs some changes.

Are the changes that I have suggested and outlined in this book the right ones? I do not really know if they are or not, but I know things need to change.

I now that I am not the only citizen of this wonderful country that is frustrated and is tired of getting the short end of the stick. We have too much disparity between the have and the have-nots in this country.

There will be those that say these words are nothing but empty rhetoric with no basis, a flight of fantasy, an exaggeration on the best of days.

Sometimes it does feel like those in the 1% do not want additional company, they do not want educated and well versed average citizens, they do not want a strong and thriving middle class. If this is not the case then now is the time to walk the walk and stop just talking about the issue. Now is the time to make a difference and make the changes today that need to be made and can not wait for a continuous stream of tomorrows that will just never end.

So you can call me a dreamer, you can call me uneducated in the way the real world works, you can call me all sorts of horrible names, you can call me foolish and childlike in my understanding of life.

Or, you can call me a citizen of the greatest country in the world, the United States of America, who is crying out for help. Begging for change, so that he and his family can prosper while feeling safe and secure.

So that all of the citizens of this great country, their children and so on, can prosper and feel safe and secure.

To those professional politicians out there, please stop making this about yourself or your party. Please put us ahead of those petty issues, please give us the opportunity to thrive once again. Let us have confidence in you again!

Special Acknowledgement

Thank you to my wife for all of your encouragement to write this book, this has truly been something I have wanted to do for a very long time.

I would also like to say thank you to those of you who have the passion to stand up for what you feel is right and do so in constructive ways and without the need for violence.

Also a huge thanks to those who have served, do serve and will serve in our military and those that have given the ultimate sacrifice to help assure we get to have the freedoms we enjoy now. Without your efforts I would not have the chance to write this book, I would not have the chance to try and make a small difference in something I feel so strongly about for our country and neither would any other citizen that agrees or disagrees with the systems and laws we have in place. Thank you!

www.ingramcontent.com/pod-product-compliance
Lightning Source LLC
Chambersburg PA
CBHW050418290526
45786CB00003B/1312